Woody's Week

Written by Michaela Morgan
Illustrated by Dee Shulman

Collins

On Monday I was happy.

On Tuesday I was sad.

love
from
Gran x

5

On Wednesday I was happy.

On Thursday I was CROSS!!!

On Friday I had an idea.

9

On Saturday I made my house.

11

On Sunday we played with my house!

13

Woody's Week

Monday

Tuesday

Friday

Saturday

Wednesday

Thursday

Sunday

Ideas for guided reading

Learning objectives: To track the text in the right order; to use a variety of cues when reading; to re-read a text to practise context cues to help read unfamiliar words; to recognise the critical features of words, e.g. shape, length, spelling pattern; to retell stories, ordering events using story language

Curriculum links: Personal, social and emotional development: Respond to experiences showing a range of feelings

Interest words: sad, cross, idea, happy, house, days of the week

High frequency words: I, was, on, it, we, played, my

Resources: whiteboards and pens

Word Count: 46

Getting started

- Look at the cover together and ask children to point out the title, the author's and illustrator's names and the blurb.
- Ask them to look at the picture and to discuss who Woody is and what the story is about. Then read the blurb together.
- Concentrate on reading Woody's expression and discuss why and where he appears happy.
- Walk through the book up to p13 and ask the children to say how Woody is feeling in each picture. Ask them to think of words to describe his feelings.
- Ask children to point out days of the week, and write them out on whiteboard.

Reading and responding

- Ask children to read aloud and independently up to p13, and observe, prompt and praise each child, intervening where necessary.
- Prompt children to remember days of the week when reading, including looking at the pictures of the calendar, or what day was on the previous page, if they are having difficulties.